Our Family Our Legacy

by

Dr. Yasir Qadhi

Published by:

Unit No. E-10, 5 Jln SS 15/4G, Subang Square,
47500 Subang Jaya, Selangor, Malaysia
+603-5612-2407 (office) / +6017-399-7411 (mobile)
info@tertib.press
www.tertib.press
@tertibpress (Facebook & Instagram)

Author	:	Dr Yasir Qadhi
Transcriber & Editor	:	Norashikin Azizan
Cover design	:	Abdul Adzim Md Daim
Book design	:	Abdul Adzim Md Daim

OUR FAMILY OUR LEGACY

First Edition: January 2023

Contents

Introduction

*A*lhamdulillāh, we praise Allah s.w.t. who knows what the heart conceals, and what the tongue does not reveal. We praise Allah s.w.t. for all that He has blessed us with. We praise Allah s.w.t. for having guided us to Islam, for having sent down to us the best of revelation and sent to us His finest of creation and guided us by His invitation to be in the believing congregation. And we send *salawat salam* upon whom Allah s.w.t. has chosen to be *Rahmatan lil 'Alamin*, the one whom even his opponents called *as-Sadiq al-Amin*, the one who will be our intercessor, our *shafa'ah* in *Yawm ad-din*. As to what follows, our topic today has the utmost importance for all of us; it is the topic of family. And I will divide this book into two sections. The first will deal with the spouse and the rights of a husband and wife and some practical tips about overcoming marital strife and having a harmonious marriage. The second part is about children and some practical tips about raising our children given the difficult environment and times we live in. And of course, the caveat must be said that time is always limited and this topic is an extremely long one. But just because we don't have months and weeks to do it, that doesn't mean that we are going to do nothing in our evenings. Whatever we cannot obtain in totality, the Arabs would say, "should not be left in totality either." Just because you cannot get all of the knowledge, it doesn't mean that you shouldn't get some knowledge either.

Yasir Qadhi

Spouses

Garments to Your Spouse

There is a beautiful metaphor that Allah s.w.t. mentions in the Qur'an about marriage.

$$\text{هُنَّ لِبَاسٌ لَّكُمْ وَأَنتُمْ لِبَاسٌ لَّهُنَّ}$$

hunna libāsul lakum wa antum libāsul lahunn

They are a clothing for you and you are a clothing for them (al-Baqarah, 2:187)

They are a clothing for you and you are a clothing for them. You, the husbands, are the clothes of your wives. You, the wives, are the clothes of your husbands. What is the implication of this metaphor? Why does Allah s.w.t. mention our spouse as our clothing? Let us ask ourselves the primary function of a garment.

Protects that which is embarrassing

The primary purpose of a garment is that it protects that which is embarrassing. Something shameful; that you don't show to the public. So the number one purpose of a spouse is to protect the faults and the hidden aspects of the other spouse. The spouse does not expose, the spouse does not shame, and the spouse does not reveal secrets that are going to embarrass his or her spouse. That is why we are the garments of our spouses. We cover that which is embarrassing.

Protects us from extreme weather

What else do our clothes and garments do? The second thing that our clothes and garments do is that they protect us from the elements which are surrounding us. So, in hot weather, you wear a certain type of clothing. In cold weather, you wear another type of clothing. In dusty weather, you wear something else. In a battle, you would wear something else that is suited for that surrounding as well. Your clothes are relevant to your context and it protects you from the context that you are in. Therefore, the understanding of the verse is that each spouse will shape themselves to protect their spouse given the circumstances that they are in. It may be that one spouse needs to be extra patient during challenging times; to have fortitude in facing difficulties or to be encouraging to the other spouse when the going gets tough, just like the garments in our wardrobe—fitting to the weather that we are in. Every one of us has a wardrobe that changes depending on the outside climate. Allah s.w.t. has said we are the garments to the other spouse. Why? To make sure that the other spouse is protected. When they need comfort, we comfort them, and when they need support, we support them and when they need courage, we encourage them.

Makes us feel complete

What else does clothing do? Clothes make us feel complete. Let's be honest, without clothing we are literally naked. We feel empty.

A spouse completes who we are. A spouse makes us feel more full. That is why the default in the children of Adam a.s. is marriage. The Prophet s.a.w. said,

> "Nikaḥ is from my methodology. So whoever wants to follow my methodology should get married. Whoever abandons marriage thinking they would get closer to Allah s.w.t., has abandoned my methodology." (Sunan ibn Majah 1486)

When Allah s.w.t. created our father, Adam a.s., Allah blessed him with Hawwa'. This is a profound point. Even before Allah s.w.t. blessed Adam a.s. with *Jannah*, Allah s.w.t. blessed him with his wife, Hawwa'. Just imagine that even *Jannah* would have been empty without a life partner.

وَقُلْنَا يَـٰٓآدَمُ ٱسْكُنْ أَنتَ وَزَوْجُكَ ٱلْجَنَّةَ...

Wa qulnā yā ādamuskun anta wa zaujukal-jannah

And We said, "O' Adam, dwell, you and your wife, in Paradise..." (al-Baqarah, 2:35)

The *zawjah*, Hawwa' has already entered *Jannah*. Even *Jannah* is incomplete without your other half—what about in this *dunya* then? That is why the default for the children of Adam a.s.—all of them—is marriage. This is something that goes back to all societies and all cultures; a life partner. Somebody who will take care of you and comfort you. Somebody that will be your other half and the one whom you can share your thoughts with. As our Prophet s.a.w. said, "Women are the twin halves of men." Women and men are on the same team, working together but having different tasks and each one is needed for the team to function.

Decorates and beautifies us

What else does a garment do? A garment also beautifies you. It also makes you feel nice. It is something you wear as *zina*. Allah s.w.t. says in the Qur'an:

يَٰبَنِىٓ ءَادَمَ خُذُواْ زِينَتَكُمْ عِندَ كُلِّ مَسْجِدٍ

Yā banī ādama khudhū zīnatakum ʿinda kulli masjid.

O' children of Adam, take your adornment [i.e., wear your clothing] at every masjid. (al-Aʿraf, 7:31)

Wear your best *zina* or adornment, when you are performing your worship. Naturally, if we have a fancy engagement, we would wear good clothes. If we are going to visit the Prime Minister or the President, we would wear nice clothes. Thus, Allah is saying, that when we go to the *masjid* we should also wear good and nice clothes. Don't put on your tattered, stinky yoga pants when you go to pray. Don't wear shorts that are not clean. No! Therefore, put on your best dress for the *masjid*.

As Allah calls our spouse as garments, we should understand that a spouse should be responsible to make us feel good, comfortable and joyful about living as what *zina* or adornment suggests.

Spouses as Signs of Allah's Existence and Miracles

وَمِنْ ءَايَـٰتِهِۦٓ أَنْ خَلَقَ لَكُم مِّنْ أَنفُسِكُمْ أَزْوَٰجًا لِّتَسْكُنُوٓا۟ إِلَيْهَا وَجَعَلَ بَيْنَكُم مَّوَدَّةً وَرَحْمَةً ۚ إِنَّ فِى ذَٰلِكَ لَـَٔايَـٰتٍ لِّقَوْمٍ يَتَفَكَّرُونَ ﴿٢١﴾

wa min āyātihī an khalaqa lakum min anfusikum azwājal litaskunū ilaihā wa ja'ala bainakum mawaddataw wa raḥmah, inna fī dhālika la 'āyātil liqaumiy yatafakkarun

And of His signs is that He created for you from yourselves mates that you may find tranquillity in them, and He placed between you affection and mercy. Indeed in that are signs for a people who give thought. (ar-Rum, 30:21)

Allah s.w.t. mentions in the Qur'an, that of His miracles and the proof of His existence; whenever Allah says, *wa min āyātihī,* we shall translate this as the proof of Allah's existence.

The verse above is a very profound verse. Allah says, "*Wa min āyātihī*" means "*and of the miracles that prove He exists*".

"*Khalaqa lakum min anfusikum*"—He created for you, from you. What did Allah create? *Azwajan.* Spouses.

There is the title of a very famous book, and it is a very good book—Men Are From Mars, Women Are From Venus. I encourage all of you to read it. But remember that Allah is emphasising that men and women are both from the Earth. They are from us. Again, "*Khalaqa lakum min anfusikum*" Allah has created for you, from you. There are some of Allah's existence that are asexual; like the amoeba. Like a one-cell organism. There are some of Allah's creations that do not have mates and do not have pairs. If Allah wanted to, He could have made us like that as well—where one person will have within themselves the mechanism to breed more than one. This exists in some aspects of the plant and animal kingdom. But Allah is saying that "No, I want to prove to you that I exist, that I care about you, that I love you. I want to prove to you that I am your Rabb. *Wa min āyātihī.*" Can you imagine if the world is asexual? Can you imagine if we didn't have life partners? Can you imagine if there weren't two genders who are attracted to one another and get married and have a family—children? Can you imagine how dreary, boring and difficult life could be?

For You, From You

You are not an alien species to one another, even though sometimes you might think that is the case. Every one of us comes from a male and a female. Every one of us has experience in interacting with both genders. Allah s.w.t. created both men and women and He is emphasising that the commonality between the two is much more than their differences—*Khalaqa lakum min anfusikum.*

Our mother, Hawwa' was created from Adam a.s. Scholars have mentioned the symbolism of being created from the rib as very powerful. However, we have no knowledge of how Allah created Hawwa' from the side of Adam a.s. But, we can clearly see the symbolism of the rib based on scholars; Hawwa' was not created from the head—so that men would glorify her, nor was she created from the feet—so that men would dominate over her. Instead, she was created from the side so that she can be with Adam a.s. and from the area of the heart so that there can be love between them. That is one of the symbolisms of the creation of women from the side of men—*Khalaqa lakum min anfusikum azjāwal litaskunū ilaihā*—so that you may find peace from them. *Litaskunū ilayhā wa ja'ala bainakum mawaddataw raḥmah.* Each spouse in a good marriage, finds *sakinah,* in the other spouse.

The ideal marriage in human history is the marriage of Prophet Muḥammad s.a.w. and Siti Khadijah r.a. We see over and over again how much the Prophet s.a.w. needed Sayyidatina Khadijah r.a. We often see the role of Khadijah and that is why Khadijah is considered to be one of the greatest women in all of human history.

Wa ja ʿala bainakum mawaddataw wa raḥmah, Allah mentions that He places two things between spouses—*mawaddah* and *raḥmah*. *Mawaddah* in the Arabic language is a special type of love. In the Arabic language, there are more than ten nouns for love. Compared to the Arabic language, the English language, on the other hand, is a very superficial language. It has only one word for love. The same word is used to describe the love of a father for a son, the love of a daughter for a mother, the love of man for wealth and money, the love of a person for their pets; dogs and cats, the love of God, and the love of the opposite gender. Everything is love. In Arabic, there are at least ten different nouns for different types of love.

For example in the story of Yusuf a.s., as mentioned in *surah* Yusuf verse 30, "*Qad shaghafahā ḥubbān.*" She had *shaghaf* for Yusuf a.s. *Shaghaf* is a lustful and sensual love. There is no such word equivalent to this in the English language. You have to say, *lustful* love. In Arabic, it is called *shaghaf*. *Mawaddah* on the other hand is a love that is tender;

a love that is nurturing, protecting and caring. And so, Allah s.w.t. says that He has placed in the heart of the spouses, *mawaddah*: a tender love; and *raḥmah:* compassion.

Inna fī dhālika la ʾāyātil liqaumiy yatafakkaṛun: Indeed in that are signs for a people who give thought. Isn't this amazing? That two people who have never interacted with each other meet one another and they start courting in a week or two or a month. Their families meet each other. And then, they get married. And the love between these two strangers becomes so powerful than any love they have ever known in their lives. Isn't it amazing? How can you love someone whom you have never known for thirty years of your life? In the twenty-five years of your life, you have never met them. But then, a marriage takes place. Allah s.w.t. mentions that "It is from my miracles and signs."

Obviously, in the ideal marriage, tenderness and compassion should exist but sometimes, unfortunately, it does not exist, and that is the *qadr* of Allah s.w.t. Hence, what is the goal? That *mawaddah* and *raḥmah* should exist. Where does it come from and how is it humanly possible to love a stranger that you did not know your whole life? How to love them with such tenderness and compassion? To sacrifice everything for her and she too sacrificing everything for him? How is it possible? Allah said, "I put it there", *Wa ja ʿala bainakum.* Because without that love, marriage will not succeed. We all know this. Without that tenderness and compassion, divorce will be looming on the horizon. It is almost impossible to save a marriage that is completely lost of *mawaddah* and *raḥmah*.

So Allah is saying in the verse, "I created those feelings within you so that life becomes easier for you." So spouses and marriage, are gifts of Allah to us. That proves Allah's power and existence and they are meant to make life easier. This is what the Qur'an is telling us. This whole *dunya* is a temporary enjoyment. You are not going to enjoy it forever. But what would you enjoy forever? It is the *akhirah*.

يَـٰقَوْمِ إِنَّمَا هَـٰذِهِ ٱلْحَيَوٰةُ ٱلدُّنْيَا مَتَـٰعٌ وَإِنَّ ٱلْـَٔاخِرَةَ هِىَ دَارُ ٱلْقَـرَارِ ﴿٣٩﴾

Innamā hādhihil-ḥayātud-dunyā matā'un wainnal-ākhirati hiya dārul-qarār

O' my people, this worldly life is only [temporary] enjoyment, and indeed, the Hereafter - that is the home of [permanent] settlement. (Ghafir, 40:39)

Dunya is *mata'*. *Mata'* means for a while. Anything that you enjoy is temporary. The pleasures of the world are temporary. Of course, *'ibadah* will be a pleasure of the hereafter which is something else. But in this *dunya*, everything is temporary. Our Prophet s.a.w. said:

> "The world is but a (quick passing) enjoyment, and the best enjoyment of the world is a pious and virtuous woman". [Muslim] (Riyaḍ aṣ-Ṣaliḥin 280)

Nothing is more blessed than that enjoyment. So, we have to ask ourselves then, what are some of the ways that we can maximise in obtaining that *mawaddah* and *rahmaḥ*— that love that Allah s.w.t. has gifted for the successful marriage? We have to remember that marriage is a continuous work in progress. We have to always work for it.

Gender Role is a Human Construct?

So what are some of the things that we need to understand? I begin by stating in contrast to some versions of modern feminism since some of them claim that there should not be any difference between men and women. That the roles of the genders are the same.

In every single culture of every civilisation, and every era of humanity, men and women have had different roles to play, except in the last decades or so—as in some societies in the West, there is a notion that men and women have no differences whatsoever. This is biologically, physically, physiologically, emotionally, historically, and *Qur'anicly*, incorrect.

Allah s.w.t. says in the Qur'an in *surah* Ali-'Imran verse 36, *"Wa laysadh-dhakaru kal unthā"* which means "and the male is not like the female." It is such a simple verse yet it destroys some strands of third-wave feminism. Basically, men are definitely not like the women. Do we need to be told about this? Yes, these days we do. The thing is, the new notion nowadays is that gender itself is a human construct. Thirty years ago, gender role was a human construct; a social construct. This means that the roles we assign to each gender are imaginary—they do not really exist.

These days, the genders themselves have become human constructs. You are now allowed to identify yourself as a different gender than your biological chromosome or your private parts. This reminds me of a saying from the Arabs, something that they would say which is, *"If you have to prove the brightness of the sun, then what uses of any evidence?"* In other words, whatever arguments you have against people are pointless. If you have to prove that the sun is bright, then you have lost your means of arguing.

Now, something that is blatantly obvious requires proof. Allah knew that mankind would go berserk about this, so Allah revealed this verse in *surah* Ali-ʿImran: *dhakaru kal unthā*—the man is not like the woman. This statement makes some people a bit sensitive, and they would then ask, "What do you mean?", "Does this means that men are better than women?" "Does this mean men are superior?" and so on which raises the issue of chauvinism and misogynism.

We can answer these questions in a very simple manner which is by quoting one simple *ḥadith* that is narrated in Jamiʿ at-Tirmidhi and Tafsir at-Tabari books. Umm Salamah, the wife of the Prophet s.a.w., said to the Prophet s.a.w., "O' Messenger of Allah, why does the Qur'an always mention men and not women? Why does the Qur'an speak in the masculine? Where is the feminine? Why aren't women mentioned in the Qur'an?"

We have to realise that the default pronoun used in the Qur'an is the masculine pronoun. Like various other languages, the Arabic language has feminine and masculine pronouns, verbs and adjectives. Generally speaking, when there is a verse in the Qur'an, it is in the masculine form. Therefore, Allah s.w.t. answers Umm Salamah's questions by revealing not one, but three verses which we recite to this day. One of the verses is on the last page of *surah* Ali-'Imran.

فَٱسْتَجَابَ لَهُمْ رَبُّهُمْ أَنِّى لَآ أُضِيعُ عَمَلَ عَـٰمِلٍ مِّنكُم مِّن ذَكَرٍ أَوْ أُنثَىٰ ۖ بَعْضُكُم مِّنْ بَعْضٍ ۖ فَٱلَّذِينَ هَاجَرُوا۟ وَأُخْرِجُوا۟ مِن دِيَـٰرِهِمْ وَأُوذُوا۟ فِى سَبِيلِى وَقَـٰتَلُوا۟ وَقُتِلُوا۟ لَأُكَفِّرَنَّ عَنْهُمْ سَيِّـَٔاتِهِمْ وَلَأُدْخِلَنَّهُمْ جَنَّـٰتٍ تَجْرِى مِن تَحْتِهَا ٱلْأَنْهَـٰرُ ثَوَابًا مِّنْ عِندِ ٱللَّهِ ۗ وَٱللَّهُ عِندَهُۥ حُسْنُ ٱلثَّوَابِ ﴿١٩٥﴾

And their Lord responded to them, "Never will I allow to be lost the work of [any] worker among you, whether male or female; you are of one another.

So those who emigrated or were evicted from their homes or were harmed in My cause or fought or were killed—I will surely remove from them their misdeeds, and I will surely admit them to gardens beneath which rivers flow as reward from Allah, and Allah has with Him the best reward. (Ali-'Imran, 3:195)

Allah responded to the questions by saying that He shall not cause the deeds of any of us, male or female, to go to waste. Each one of us is from the other. So both men and women who believe, make sacrifices and do good deeds, shall get *Jannah*. In our religion, we say unequivocally and unabashedly that men and women are spiritually equal in front of Allah s.w.t. and that is *real equality*. Being born a certain gender does not make someone at a disadvantage in the eyes of Allah and in earning the pleasure of Allah s.w.t. This is the real equality we strive for. **Islam is the first faith and philosophy in humanity to make men and women equal.** In terms of spirituality and humanity they are both on par and that is real equality. **However, it is also important to note that each gender's role and responsibility are complementary**. Each one is assigned to what is more suited to do.

The problem with third-wave feminism, in particular,

or to a lesser degree, second-wave feminism; is that they prioritise the roles and tasks of men to be superior. Once they have given a superior value to the tasks of men, then automatically and intrinsically they determine that the roles of women are inferior. The problem lies in their own imaginary valuation.

The above verse 195 of *surah* Ali-'Imran mentions, *ba'dukum min ba'd*—you are of one another. Every one of you comes from the other. There is no superiority of worth. Both men and women have their share of tasks. Each one has a share of tasks, responsibilities, inheritance—basically everything. When it comes to the task of this *dunya*, such as family roles and responsibilities in society, there will be differences. There are certain tasks that Allah s.w.t. has assigned to one gender and certain tasks to the other and there is no aspect of superiority or demeaning between these two roles.

Problems rise when we consider one role to be better than the other. Let me give you a simple example that will help illustrate this point better. There is a pair of twins who went through high school together. Let's say, they got the exact same grade. One twin went to the college of engineering, and the other twin went to the college of medicine. So, they are twins and they have the same DNA, gender, IQ, and grades. They spend four or five years in different specialities. When they finish, do you think it would be logical or reasonable that the one who graduated from engineering says, "Hey that's not fair, you get to be in the operation theatre? You get to do surgeries, that's not fair. Why do you get to do surgeries? I want to do surgeries too. I am someone who is just like you as well." And do you think it will be wise if the twin doctor says the same thing? "Hey, that's not fair, you're solving quadratic equations, you're at the engineering plant. I want to do that as well!"

If you can understand that four years of training makes different people suited for different tasks, then you can think that everyone is designed for different tasks. We all have our differences in our DNA, in our XY and XX chromosomes. There are differences in our physical, physiological, emotional and logical differences and even body differences. Of course, because of the differences, there should be different tasks that each of us needs to carry out.

A society cannot function properly without engineers or doctors. Each has a role to play. The engineers need doctors and the doctors need engineers. This is a simple example that applies to the roles in society. How about the roles of men and women, husbands and wives and mothers and fathers? As I mentioned, the problem is when we take a role and make it better than the other. No, it is not. With that caveat, let us mention some of the rights and responsibilities that the Qur'an and *sunnah* constitute. We will start with the rights that the husband has over the wife and the rights that the wives have over their husbands.

Hierarchy is Not Nobility

وَٱلْمُطَلَّقَـٰتُ يَتَرَبَّصْنَ بِأَنفُسِهِنَّ ثَلَـٰثَةَ قُرُوٓءٍ ۚ وَلَا يَحِلُّ لَهُنَّ أَن يَكْتُمْنَ مَا خَلَقَ ٱللَّهُ فِىٓ أَرْحَامِهِنَّ إِن كُنَّ يُؤْمِنَّ بِٱللَّهِ وَٱلْيَوْمِ ٱلْءَاخِرِ ۚ وَبُعُولَتُهُنَّ أَحَقُّ بِرَدِّهِنَّ فِى ذَٰلِكَ إِنْ أَرَادُوٓاْ إِصْلَـٰحًا ۚ وَلَهُنَّ مِثْلُ ٱلَّذِى عَلَيْهِنَّ بِٱلْمَعْـرُوفِ ۚ وَلِلرِّجَـالِ عَلَيْهِـنَّ دَرَجَـةٌ ۗ وَٱللَّـهُ عَزِيـزٌ حَكِيـمٌ ﴿٢٢٨﴾

Divorced women remain in waiting [i.e., do not remarry] for three periods, and it is not lawful for them to conceal what Allah has created in their wombs if they believe in Allah and the Last Day. And their husbands have more right to take them back in this [period] if they want reconciliation. And due to them [i.e., the wives] is similar to what is expected of them, according to what is reasonable. But the men [i.e., husbands] have a degree over them [in responsibility and authority]. And Allah is Exalted in Might and Wise. (Ali-'Imran, 3:228)

Allah says in the Qur'an very explicitly that women have rights due to them, rights which are similar to the rights that the husbands can ask from their wives. This is a very simple, beautiful and powerful verse. There is a similar amount from the women that is expected from them to the men. Similar but not the same. Similar here means that each one has rights and responsibilities but not the same obligations and responsibilities.

$$ وَلِلرِّجَالِ عَلَيْهِنَّ دَرَجَةٌ $$

But the men [i.e., husbands] have a degree over them [in responsibility and authority].

And then Allah says, which might seem to be a contradiction but obviously it is not. And men have one *darajah* over them. This is such a profound verse because Allah began the verse by saying, "Hey, the both of you are equal." And then in the middle Allah says, "But men have one degree over them." How is that possible? How can the Qur'an say that both are equal and each one has due upon them a similar to what they must be given? And then Allah says, "But men have one *darajah*."

Notice this. Allah uses a beautiful word, *darajah*. And *darajah*, if you speak Arabic you would know that it is in the *nakirah* form, it is the smallest manner. We can translate this as saying, "But men have one degree over them. Just a little bit over them." How and why is this? Because at the end of the day, two people cannot equally run a business, a corporation, or an entity. There has to be a hierarchy. Now, this is extremely important. *Hierarchy does not imply nobility.* Hierarchy is simply management, *not superiority.* This is the key that, unfortunately, most third-wave feminists do not understand.

Every one of us submits to a hierarchy in every aspect of our life. Do we not pull over when the police are telling us to pull over? There is a hierarchy there. The police have authority over us. Do we believe that the police are superior than ordinary human beings? Nobody believes this, right actually? The government has a hierarchy. Does it have superiority? No. In your workplace or corporation, you do not expect to be treated like the CEO. You do not expect to be treated like your boss. Instead, you report to your boss. Sometimes your boss is better than you as a human being, and sometimes he is worse than you as a human being. But the main point I am iterating is that hierarchy is not the same as nobility. In order for a corporation to run, there has to be a hierarchy. Can you imagine if every employee would just barge in and say, "Hey, why don't you treat me like the CEO? I should have the right to tell you what to do." Can you imagine if every employee did that? What would happen then? The entire corporation will collapse. In order to run anything, there must be a hierarchy.

When it comes to marriage, Allah s.w.t. says, "The two of you are joined together. But if push comes to shove, if one has to, in the end, have a say; then men have one degree over them." This hierarchy as we say does not imply superiority or nobility. It is very possible that in your corporation, an employee lower than you might be more pious than you, he might be placed higher in *Jannah* than you. Just because you are the boss, it does not make you better than other people. But the company must run and you must be the boss because you need to lead. If you are a boss at a good company then that perhaps shows that you are qualified in what you are doing.

Thus, in relation to the example, Allah s.w.t. is similarly saying, for a family to run biologically, physically, physiologically, and emotionally, the man is tasked with a job that is slightly different from the woman's, which is suited for him. And the woman too has a slighly different job or task, which is suitable for her. The more explicit verse is the one from *surah* an-Nisa'. Allah s.w.t. says in the Qur'an:

ٱلرِّجَالُ قَوَّٰمُونَ عَلَى ٱلنِّسَآءِ بِمَا فَضَّلَ ٱللَّهُ بَعْضَهُمْ عَلَىٰ بَعْضٍ وَبِمَآ أَنفَقُوا مِنْ أَمْوَٰلِهِمْ ۚ فَٱلصَّٰلِحَٰتُ قَٰنِتَٰتٌ حَٰفِظَٰتٌ لِّلْغَيْبِ بِمَا حَفِظَ ٱللَّهُ ۚ وَٱلَّٰتِى تَخَافُونَ نُشُوزَهُنَّ فَعِظُوهُنَّ وَٱهْجُرُوهُنَّ فِى ٱلْمَضَاجِعِ وَٱضْرِبُوهُنَّ ۖ فَإِنْ أَطَعْنَكُمْ فَلَا تَبْغُوا عَلَيْهِنَّ سَبِيلًا ۗ إِنَّ ٱللَّهَ كَانَ عَلِيًّا كَبِيرًا ۝

Men are in charge of women by [right of] what Allah has given one over the other and what they spend [for maintenance] from their wealth. So righteous women are devoutly obedient, guarding in [the husband›s] absence what Allah would have them guard. But those [wives] from whom you fear arrogance - [first] advise them; [then if they persist], forsake them in bed; and [finally], strike them [lightly]. But if they obey you [once more], seek no means against them. Indeed, Allah is ever Exalted and Grand. (an-Nisa', 4:34)

Men are *qawwam* over women. Allah s.w.t. gave two reasons for that—one that is inherent in them and one that is acquired subsequently, and said: 'because Allah has made one of them to excel the other', and 'because they spend (to support them) from their means' which refers to what they spend with regard to marriage—such as the *mahr* and maintenance.

These are all gender roles in the Qur'an. Anyone who says that there is no such thing as gender roles has not read the Qur'an. They are not coming from a Muslim frame of mind then. They are not understanding the Qur'an then. The Qur'an is very explicit: there are gender roles ipso facto there are genders as well. By the way, philosophically, when Western societies negate gender roles, it is inevitable that they would negate genders. When gender roles became meaningless thirty years ago, the next step was that genders would become meaningless. It is an inevitable flow, and that is why dear Muslims, do not jump on the liberal bandwagon, do not jump on secular humanism, it is philosophically and morally bankrupt. It is not going to give you happiness in this *dunya*, much less in *akhirah*. Look at what is happening in the Western world; depression, suicide, marital disruption, crime, and drugs. When you have a child but they do not grow up in a marriage, then the child is not going to have a role model. Plenty of surveys and studies have shown that children from single homes and single parents' marriages and households are more prone to violence. They are more prone to drugs and crime. Growing up in a stable family is one of the biggest impediments to becoming a thief. If somebody is raised in a stable home—regardless of their faith—their environment generally creates a stable child.

Rights of a Husband

My point is back to what we were saying: Allah s.w.t. says in the Qur'an, *Arrijālu qawwāmūna 'alal-nisā'*. Let us now translate what *qawwam* means. Men are *qawwam* over women. *Qawwam is* from the same word as *qaʾim*; meaning standing. *Qaʾim* means to stand. And *qawwam* has the indication and connotation that the man is standing up, looking out, and protecting and sheltering the woman. The verse does not translate to men being the bosses of women. No! The primary meaning is that men are the protectors and maintainers of women. This is what *qawwam* means to men; you have to take care of your wife. This is what Allah is saying, that you men are responsible for protecting them (women).

Just imagine, a tribe huddling together and a strong person looking out for the enemy. That strong person is the brave one, he is taking the arrows. That person is putting himself in danger, to protect the ones who are sitting down. That is what *qawwam* means. The man who sacrifices his life for his wife and children. This is true manhood in Islam. And the brutal fact that matters is that Allah s.w.t. created men to be *qawwam* and He created women who love a man that is a *qawwam*. What woman would not like her husband to protect her, nourish her, and care for her? Allah created women that way. A true man, a true *rajul* is somebody who has that sense of protection. "I will take care of her, I will sacrifice for her, I will dedicate my life, my *rizq*, my earnings and my career, all of it, for the sake of my family." This applies whether you are a Muslim or not. That is how Allah created men. And that is why when the Western society is changing this matter, men are becoming effeminate and women are becoming emasculate. Society is going completely corrupt. It is just not going to function this way.

My point is that Allah s.w.t. is very explicit about what is the main gender roles and *qiwamah*. *Qiwamah* means protection, maintenance and nourishment. Think of the hunter-gatherer relationship. By the way, another point I would like to mention here is that feminism would never have come if the Industrial Revolution had not taken place. There would be no such thing as feminism if we had to go fight for our food, forage in the desert, and protect our territories the way most societies did. Feminism can only come in societies where much of what men used to do is no longer done. We thank Allah s.w.t. that the world is a safer place. But it is because of these industrialisations and now, of course, computers and networks have further sparked this matter. Fair enough, the playing field for women has been levelled to a great extent but it is not 100%. The most difficult jobs are still always done by men. For example, miners; there are no female miners because a woman does not go digging a thousand feet under. Even in the deep sea. There are scuba divers whose careers are living in little bubbles and submarines for months on end and it is extremely dangerous and most are men. The armies around the world as well have at least 70 to 80 per cent or in some countries, 100% of whom are men. Firefighters, almost all are invariably men. You cannot change certain aspects of *qiwamah*. This is what a man does, he protects, he sacrifices, and he struggles. Allah created men that way. They can do it. So, of the tasks assigned to men is that of *qiwamah*. Now, with *qiwamah* comes a little element of respect as well. This element is not superiority, it is simply hierarchy. So, it is also correct to say that *qawwam* does have a whiff of having to take charge. This is also an undeniable meaning of *qiwamah*. So those who read in a notion of hierarchy in this verse are also correct. Allah also explains *qawwam* over women and Allah gives two reasons:

$$\text{بِمَا فَضَّلَ ٱللَّهُ بَعْضَهُمْ عَلَىٰ بَعْضٍ}$$

Allah has given one over the other

This is biology. One has been given certain things the other has not been given. For example, physical strength. Even in the Olympics, to this date, men and women do not compete with each other side by side. Almost in every single world record in regards to speed, agility—men are a little bit more than women. Allah is saying that men are given certain biological things that women do not have. One of them is physical strength. The average man is physically taller than the average woman. The average man is stronger than the average woman. This is an undeniable reality. We can also add to this list: fortitude, stamina, and courage. There is nothing wrong with this nor does this mean men are better than women. The differences are not something that we should find as a joking or trivial matter. For example, women generally are terrified of certain things men are not terrified of like cockroaches. My point here is that there is nothing to find funny about this at all. Why? Let's get to the other side; what a woman can do with rearing the children, *subḥānAllāh*. Men are in awe looking at women accomplishing these tasks. They could not even do a fraction of it.

وَبِمَآ أَنفَقُوا۟ مِنْ أَمْوَٰلِهِمْ

And what they spend [for maintenance] from their wealth.

The second point: *wabimā anfaqū min amwālihim*—And because it is the men that have to spend their money on the women. In our religion, a woman—in an ideal situation—is never obliged to spend a penny. When she is born, her father is responsible for her. If the father has died, the brother takes charge. When she gets married, her husband is going to pay for her food, her maintenance, her house, and her clothing. When her husband dies, her son will take care of her before he can take care of his wife. From birth to death, in an ideal family situation, a woman is taken care of. Whereas, in an ideal situation of a man—a man has to stand on his own feet, has to have his own job, and take care of himself. Hence, the father should encourage the son at a young age to get a job as soon as the son is able. That is what a man does. So Allah is saying, *wabimā anfaqū min amwālihim*, and because men are spending their wealth upon women.

Dear sisters, have you ever realised, that on average, 70% to 90% of a husband's income is spent on his family? Have you ever thought about that? Rent, groceries, education, and the expenses that are spent for the household. On average across the globe, 70% to 90% of lower-middle and upper-middle-class man's income goes to their wife and children. *Wabimā anfaqū min amwālihim.*

There is something known as The Golden Rule. Do unto others what you want to be done unto you. This is the politically correct version of The Golden Rule. There is a *politically incorrect* version. **He who has the gold gets to make the rules**. That is the other Golden Rule. There is a humour element in that, but this is what Allah is saying; when a person is going to spend the bulk of his wealth on you, with that comes as well a little bit of privilege or hierarchy. Once again, hierarchy does not imply superiority or nobility. It is simply to keep the ship running. It is simply for the corporation to function. And Allah is saying that the average man has characteristics that make him more suited to be the CEO of the company known as the family. If the *rajul* is a true *rajul*, then they are better qualified than an average lady.

Now, I would like to also mention another vital point and it is perhaps one of the most powerful points of this book: Allah s.w.t. has assigned archetypical gender roles, i.e. in an ideal situation, men should do this. And in an ideal situation, women should do this. This is true, but reflect on this: generally speaking, those roles are ***not wajib*** and can be individually negotiated on a case-by-case basis. This is the beauty of our religion. Yes, there are archetypical ideals, in the utopia in which every man does X and every woman does Y. There is a default that should be what we strived for, and that default is *arrijālul qawwāmūnal 'ala nisa'*. But Allah did not make it obligatory if and only if the parties re-negotiate. Both parties reach a compromise. Both parties decide to do something else.

The default: the man is *qawwam*, and the man must give the money. But if for some reason, the man was in an accident, and now he is in a wheelchair and cannot do anything then there can be something else. An example would be pertaining to a friend of mine, who did a PhD in Humanities. He married his wife who is in medical school to become a doctor. And both of them are in the career stage. In America, professors are paid 1/5 of what doctors are paid. Both of them are practising Muslims and they said, 'you know, we want to raise our children on a good income, let the man become the caretaker and let the woman go and be the breadwinner.' Are they sinful? No. Why? Because Allah did not make gender roles *wajib*. Do you understand this point? This is the key point and one of the most profound points. There are defaults, but those defaults can be individually negotiated by mutual consultation. By both parties agreeing. A man cannot demand his wife to go pay the bills. She can go to the Islamic court and says, "I don't want to. That's his job." And she would win. But if both of them agree, then yes. The roles can become arbitrary. What if she is a widow, like Khadijah? She needed to work, and then she worked. What if she doesn't have any brothers? What about these kinds of situations happen? Then what? This is where we can see the beauty of the *shariʿah*. The default is there, but there is plenty of avenues for exceptions. So, as we speak about the default, let us not forget that *Alḥamdulillāh*, the *shariʿah* allows for a vast diversity depending on individual circumstances and choices as long as it is done with mutual consultation.

Now, when the man is *qawwam* over the woman, one of the main overall explicit rights that the Qurʾan and *sunnah* have come with is the right of respect; to be respected. Just like the CEO of the company. If you are dismissive and rude to the CEO, the company is not going to function properly. Even if you disagree, there is a method and mechanism to do so. To be outright contemptuous or rude in any corporation, will cause you to lose your job. Psychologically speaking, Allah created man with a massive and fragile ego. If the ego is trampled on, marriage is almost inevitably doomed.

There is a *hadith* that might make some sisters feel insulted even though they shouldn't feel like that because this is true from the aspect of human psychology.

لَوْ كُنْتُ آمِرًا أَحَدًا أَنْ يَسْجُدَ لِأَحَدٍ لَأَمَرْتُ الْمَرْأَةَ أَنْ تَسْجُدَ لِزَوْجِهَا

If I were to command anyone to prostrate to anyone
else, I would have commanded women to prostrate
to their husbands. (Jamiʿ at-Tirmidhi 1159)

It is a beautiful ḥadith narrated by Abu Hurayrah
and the beginning part is very beautiful but some sisters
might find the ending part problematic. Muʿadh ibn Jabal
returned from Syria. He was in Syria at first and then he
came back to Madinah. He entered the *masjid* after two
months of travelling and he had not seen the Prophet s.a.w.
for over two months. He entered the *masjid* and in front of
all of the *ṣahabah*, he fell down flat in *sajdah*; in front of the
Prophet s.a.w. The Prophet s.a.w. said, "Muʿadh, what are
you doing?" So Muʿadh said, "O' Messenger of Allah, I just
came back from Syria, and I saw the Christians prostrating
to their bishops. And I said to myself, if those guys can
prostrate to their bishops, then *wallāhi*, you have more rights
that we prostrate to you." And the Prophet s.a.w. said, "*La
taf ʿal*"—*Do not do this again.* It is not permissible for humans
to prostrate to another human in our *shariʿah*. Then he said
the phrase that some sisters might find problematic, but we
should not because it is human psychology. It is not *fiqh*,
it is psychology. "But if I were to have allowed anyone to
prostrate to someone else, I would have said to the wife,
that she should prostrate to her husband. Because she owes

him." This *ḥadith* is authentic in many books of *ḥadith* and once again, it tells us about the reality of human beings. Men want to have that respect from their wives. They want their wives to look up to them as *qawwam*. This is the main function to make a marriage happy.

A man wants to be *qawwam*. It is his *fitrah*, his DNA. And when the wife makes him the *qawwam*, he is the happiest husband in the world. And a part of being *qawwam* is that authority and respect. To give an element of respect to the CEO, to understand that Allah has given a worldly ranking, a hierarchy in this *dunya*, not the *akhirah*. Your husband can be an evil person in the eyes of Allah, but if he is giving you your rights, he is still the *qiwamah* of this world. He can have his private sins and he has to answer for them. But if he is giving you your rights, the concept of *qiwamah* is there. Unless they abandon your rights, then the concept goes down. The point is when the wife gives that element of *qiwamah* to the man which is to show actual and genuine respect, this empowers the man to be a better *qawwam* for his wife. He is going to work harder for his wife. He is going to protect his wife even more with love. He will give her what she wants which is love and attention. You see, Allah created men and women complementarily. What men want primarily in a marriage is the femininity of their wives, a part of which is *qiwamah*. "Give me that authority, I am the husband."

That is also why there is an entire genre of *hadith* about the bedroom and the rights of a man when he calls his wife. Many women do not understand this. It is not about the act, it is not about the conjugal relationship nor the biological activity but it is about the *qiwamah* of man. It is about the man's sense of authority. "I am asking you something and you are not giving me something. You are not giving me this intimate issue and it is a private matter between husband and wife, and you are going to deny me?" Then you are destroying the man's *qiwamah*. It is not the bedroom act, it is more about the man's sense of responsibility. "I am responsible for my wife. And if I want something in return she should give me this aspect." When the woman says, "No, I am not going to give it to you." And that is why the Prophet s.a.w. says:

Narrated Abu Hurayrah:

Allah's Messenger s.a.w. said, "If a husband calls his wife to his bed (i.e. to have sexual relation) and she refuses and causes him to sleep in anger, the angels will curse her till morning." (Ṣaḥiḥ al-Bukhari 3237)

By the way, this also means that the husband cannot force himself on her but the husband has the right to get angry.

That is also very clear because the *ḥadith* did not say, "Let him go and force himself onto her." The *ḥadith* is saying, "If the woman says no, she has to deal with the consequences." And one of those consequences is the angels will curse her, *la'nah* her all night. That is if she has no excuses. But if she has an excuse then Allah does not burden a soul beyond the limit it can bear. But the point is that it is not about the conjugal act. It is about the *qiwamah* of a man. It is about when a woman says "No." At that moment, a man is opening up and being vulnerable; soft and tender. A man is saying, "I need you on this delicate and sensitive issue." Then she scowls and turns away from him for no reason. What she has done is that she has used her femininity as a weapon. She has taken her femininity and deprived her man who is her *qiwamah* in a manner that will destroy his love, protection and feeling of *qiwamah* for her.

Again, this all goes back to psychology. That is why even non-Muslim researchers are writing books about marital issues. I have read over thirty books and have taught classes about marital intimacy and marriage in Islam; I extracted the Islamic elements and researched based on the Qur'an and *sunnah*, and every book I read says the same thing. Women should not choose the bedroom as a weapon and deprive a man of his conjugal rights because of a marital dispute. Do something else. Throw a tantrum in another manner. Get angry in a different way. But do not emotionally blackmail your husband by depriving him of what he wants when he asks you. Because once again, it goes back to the issue of *qiwamah*. In conclusion, we have established here that men are *qawwam* over women. *Qawwam* is first, protection and second, maintenance. To protect, take care of, and bring in the food. To make sure there is a roof over their heads—*qiwamah*.

Rights of a Wife

Let's flip it around. What are a wife's rights to her husband? What can she demand or expect from her husband? Once again, we go back to human psychology. What does a woman primarily want? Most men do not know this. Most men do not understand. It is one of our biggest problems in marriage. Men do not understand women and women do not understand men. Primarily, a woman wants the love and attention of her husband. She wants a special best friend. Somebody who will be there for her whenever she needs. She wants somebody who will appreciate her beauty, her femininity, to be generic, she wants love. Adoration. Admiration. That is how Allah created women. Now, when a man is made *qawwam*, he would give love to the one who has made him *qawwam*.

You see, sisters. I will tell you a secret. The fact of the matter is women have far more power in a relationship than men do. But they do not understand what that power is. A man can be reduced to pulp. A man can be tied around your little finger. A man can follow anything you want if you exert his capability in a way that your femininity requires him to do. Not in a way that masculinity is understood. And that is why another *hadith* in Ṣaḥīḥ al-Bukhari is again also found 'problematic', but honestly, there is no problematic ḥadith or ayah. It is all human psychology if you just understood it. Our Prophet s.a.w. said, the famous *hadith* of deficient in intelligence and religion—the famous *hadith*—نُقْصَانُ الْعَقْلِ وَالدِّينِ. The *hadith* is actually a praise of women, not a dismissal of them. The Prophet s.a.w. said:

It is narrated on the authority of 'Abdullah b. 'Umar that the Messenger of Allah observed:

O' womenfolk, you should give charity and ask much forgiveness for I saw you in bulk amongst the dwellers of Hell. A wise lady among them said: Why is it, Messenger of Allah, that our folk is in bulk in Hell? Upon this the Prophet observed: You curse too much and are ungrateful to your spouses. I have seen none lacking in common sense and failing in religion but (at the same time) robbing the wisdom of the wise, besides you. Upon this, the woman remarked: What is wrong with our common sense and with religion? He (the Holy Prophet) observed: Your lack of common sense (can be well judged from the fact) that the evidence of two women is equal to one man, that is proof of the lack of common sense, and you spend some nights (and days) in which you do not offer prayer and in the month of Ramadan (during the days) you do not observe fast, that is a failing in religion. (Ṣaḥīḥ Muslim 79a)

The Prophet s.a.w. said that he does not understand, how women are weaker than men, and generally speaking, how they are not as intelligent or cunning as men, and yet, they have the power to make the most intelligent man lose all his intelligent and act like a fool. This is what the *hadith* translated as.

The Prophet s.a.w. is above the problems that all of us manifest, OK? When we are in love, we are completely foolish. We lose track of reality. We do things that people just don't do. They would say something like, "How could you do something so foolish?" But that is what a man does out of love. So our Prophet s.a.w. is saying, "I don't understand women, you are not as conniving or cunning as men are and yet you have the power to take an intelligent man and reduced him to a withering fool." He was wondering how you have that power. And of course, the answer is *Allah gave you the power*. But only when you exude femininity, soft power, you know, go back to your childhood fairy tales, the motive of the damsel in distress. It is a deep psychological motive of men and women. The average man does not want to marry a woman who becomes a mother-like figure. "Why did you do this? Why are you doing that? How much do you spend money on this?" Oh my God, *lā ḥawlā walā quwwata illā billāh*. An average man would be able to last in a marriage, or even if he lasts it is not going to be a good marriage. But if the woman becomes the damsel in distress, rather than becoming the strong, masculine power which a mother should do, no problem. Because yes, we expect a mother to do that, right? But a husband does not want his wife to become a mother—a dominating figure. Rather than becoming a dominating figure, she becomes a damsel in distress. And she shows that the man is *qiwamah*. The man is the one who is the protector and the maintainer. And she does this, how? By showing the man, the *qiwamah*, the respect he wants. Sisters, if you give your husband that level of *qiwamah*, he will give you the level of love and attention you desire. He will listen to you and obey you in a way that he would never obey if you exude hard and masculine power. It does not work that way.

And so the rights that Allah s.w.t. has guaranteed are the rights that women want to be maintained, protected and taken care of. The Prophet s.a.w. said, never, ever abandon the wife. Because one of the fears in pre-modern societies, the husband just walks away. What's the woman going to do? Who's going to take care of her? The Prophet s.a.w. said, "Never abandon her." She should always have a roof over her head and that is why our Prophet s.a.w. had a marital dispute with his wives—reflect on this—even he, the Messenger of Allah—had arguments. And one month went by when he was not speaking to his wife. Even his marriage has ups and downs. When he had that argument, he went outside of the house and slept at the *masjid*. The woman is never kicked out of the house. Never. When you have an argument where you cannot be in the same room, that is *halal*. You go sleep in the living room, not her. She gets the bedroom. If it gets worse than that, you walk out the door, not her. She has protection which is her house. She has her food, she has her *rizq* and she has a roof over her head. A woman desires safety, protection and love. Allah s.w.t. guarantees that no matter what happens, you are required to take care of your wife. And again, the beauty of our religion, is that the psychological needs of each gender are enshrined in the *shari'ah*. When a woman acts like a woman, the man will treat her like a queen. And when a woman treats her husband like the *qiwamah* that he is, she will get in return, essentially a loyal servant. Essentially. She will get someone who will do everything she asks to. If she says, "Jump." He would say, "How high?" And he would do it with macho-ness, that "I am a man." But in reality, he is listening to his wife. And I shouldn't say this publicly but it is the truth. Every man knows this deep down by the way. OK? They just don't want to tell you. The power dynamics are very skewed. You have the power, sisters. Not us. But you don't understand it. You think that power is given in a hard manner. It doesn't work that way. That's it, the damsel in distress.

To Husbands and Wives...

Husbands and wives, I'll conclude on this note.

There is no such as a drama-free marriage. Every marriage has drama. Every marriage has ups and downs. If anybody would have had a drama-free marriage, it would be our Prophet s.a.w. But even he had spats. Even he had voices being raised. You need to walk into a marriage understanding the honeymoon phase is temporary. It is good, it is great. But life begins after the honeymoon. Allah blesses us with a honeymoon, which is great. So that the love is cemented, but after that, ups and downs will happen. Therefore, the love that develops after the honeymoon phase is not the love of Hollywood. Because Hollywood always finishes with "A Happily Ever After". Right? When they got married, the honeymoon began, and they lived happily after. That passionate love during the honeymoon phase is temporary, it is romanticised. It is how poems and movies are written about, no problem. But it is an illusionary love. It is not permanent love. Permanent love is a seasoned love. A weathered love. A love that has gone through thick and thin. It has gone through the problems of life and ups and downs. You love someone knowing how flawed they are. That is not the honeymoon phase as it just presents a false image of others. And that love will have ups and downs. The goal is to have more ups and downs. That is the goal.

Husbands and wives, listen to this.

The most optimistic verse in the Qur'an is the promise that Allah has said about marriage. That is if a husband and wife are fighting one another, Allah says in the Qur'an:

$$وَإِنْ خِفْتُمْ شِقَاقَ بَيْنِهِمَا فَٱبْعَثُوا۟ حَكَمًا مِّنْ أَهْلِهِۦ وَحَكَمًا مِّنْ أَهْلِهَآ إِن يُرِيدَآ إِصْلَـٰحًا يُوَفِّقِ ٱللَّهُ بَيْنَهُمَآ ۗ إِنَّ ٱللَّهَ كَانَ عَلِيمًا خَبِيرًا ﴿٣٥﴾$$

And if you fear dissension between the two, send an arbitrator from his people and an arbitrator from her people. If they both desire reconciliation, Allah will cause it between them. Indeed, Allah is ever Knowing and Aware. (an-Nisa', 4:35)

There is no more optimistic verse about marriage in the whole Qur'an. Allah guarantees if the husband and wife want to make the marriage work, Allah will bring about reconciliation and make the marriage work for them. This is a promise in the Qur'an. If the two of them want to get along and make it work, Allah will find a way to make it work. So, my conclusion point about marital issues is men, you are *qawwam* and women, you have a power that you do not realise and you give your man what he wants, which is the *qiwamah*, he will give you much more than you could ever ask for. But issues are going to happen. When issues happen, whichever party feels the pain or suffering should approach the other in a moment of calmness, not anger. Because it will never be solved if you are angry. And you should use language that is soft, and you should communicate 90% of the time because the other spouse does not understand the grievances of the other. And the assumption is; sisters in particular, "Of course, he'd understand. That's why I'm angry." Believe me, 99% of the time we have no clue why. It is because our wavelengths are different. You know the FM radio, right? We are on one frequency, and you, *masha'Allāh*, are on 15 different frequencies. We are just so narrow-minded to that frequency, OK? I say to my wife, "Speak to me like a child. Tell me what you want me to do, and I'll do it." Don't give these illusions, just tell me. What is the issue? Say it. Speak to me like a child. And Allah has blessed women with various talents; multifaceted and Allah has made men one-dimensional. You literally need to tell what the issue is. Do not ever assume, and this also goes the other way around. Don't expect your wife to understand why you are irritated and upset.

The final point is to remember to explain in soft language. I'll give you one issue in soft language. Soft language— never say you, say I. Don't say, "*You* were late." Use *I*. "*I* was worried when you didn't come. *I* didn't know where you were." Women, when you use the 'I' phrase, you become the damsel in distress. When you use the 'You' phrase, you become his mother. And you don't want to be his mother. When you say, "I was worried.", all of the sudden, your *qawwam* man will wither in front of you. "Oh, I'm so sorry." When you use the 'I' language, all of the sudden, the man understands that, "I fell short. I was supposed to protect you and I didn't do that." Whereas when you use the accusative language of 'You', automatically he becomes defensive. "Woah, you should understand me!" Automatically. The same goes for the husband. It is the same thing, it is human nature. The 'I' language rather than the 'You' language.

Children

7 Rules that We Can Apply in Raising Children

1. There are no rules.

If anyone tells you that they have 7 or 10 rules that are guaranteed will help you raise your kids properly, they are wrong. One of the famous books I read is by a person with a PhD in Psychology from Harvard, he is a child therapist. He has written books about child-raising. In the introduction, he mentioned, during his PhD at Harvard, he had six theories about how to raise children. Eventually, God blesses him with six children, and he no longer had any theories. There are no rules. And anyone who tells you that there is a hard and fast rule you can use clearly does not have children of their own. What works for one kid might not work for the other. What works on the second and third might not work on the fourth one. What works in one society might not work in the other. That is why the Qur'an and *sunnah* are not detailed manuals which prescribe specific rules on how to raise children. It is an on-the-job learning experience. You cannot read a manual on how to raise kids. You learnt and you trained as your kids are growing up. You have to be active and participate actively. So, understand that there is no magic textbook. Yes, there is general advice that I will talk about in a bit. There are no rules, but generic advice. Yes, there are things you can try but no one can tell you what to do to guarantee how the child will come out. You can do everything and still the child can be misguided. May Allah protect us from this. And you can do nothing, or everything—look at the Prophet s.a.w., an orphan child, a son of Adam a.s., who became the Messenger of Allah to help us. So there are no rules. It is trial and error. This is lead to my second *point*, not *rule*.

2. Actively Participating as A Parent

In order for anything to succeed, there must be two components. There must be anything, child-rearing is one thing. *Ikhlas* in your *niyyah*, and *'ilm*. For *ikhlas* in *niyyah*, you have to do for the sake of Allah s.w.t. You have to have a desire. And then you have to have knowledge. You are not going to be an engineer unless you want to. And then you go study engineering. You are not going to become an expert skier unless you have the desire to go skiing and you have the knowledge and you learnt the knowledge. And it really surprises me that so many parents don't even have the desire to make sure that their kids are good human beings, good Muslims, and good citizens. It is not even on their agenda. How do you expect your children to be good Muslims when it is not even on your agenda that "I want to make them good Muslims"? You are concerned about their education, the furniture of their room, the latest gadget that they own, and whether their food is organic, this is great. But what about their *iman* and *taqwa*? How about the concern for Allah s.w.t. and His love in their hearts? How about the concern of knowing who the Prophet s.a.w. is? So, if you don't even have it on your agenda and radar, what is going to happen?

So the second point is that you have to have the intention and knowledge. Knowledge means that you have to play a role in your children's lives; you have to know what is going on. Even if you make mistakes you are going to ask your cousins, your colleagues and your peers, "How did you tackle this situation?" This is knowledge. It is true that there is no one magic book but in terms of knowledge, people have experience. Knowledge is just understanding what the best techniques are. The point is you have to play an active role. An active father who sometimes fails is infinitely better than an inactive father who succeeds in the *dunya* but fails to take care of his family. Try to be loving parents even if you failed in your tactics. Eventually, your child will recognise the love even if they disagree with the tactics. We all know this from our own parents.

Looking back, maybe we even disagree with some of what they did to us—some, not all—but wisdom will teach you what they did is right. But perhaps you might say, they were too harsh back then. Now that we are older we all know that they did it because of love. We recognised that love. Hence my point number two: Nothing will get done unless you have a genuine desire, being *ikhlas* for the sake of Allah s.w.t. because indeed all actions are based on the intentions. This is mentioned in the following *ḥadith*:

> "I heard the Messenger of Allah s.a.w. say: 'Actions are but by the intention and every man will have but that which he intended. So he whose emigration was for Allah and His Messenger, his emigration was for Allah and His Messenger. But he whose emigration was for some worldly benefit or to take some woman in marriage, his emigration was for that which he migrated." (Sunan ibn Majah 4227)

As I mentioned before, playing an active role is pertinent as a parent. You have to remember that parenting is perpetual on-the-job training. It is not like you go to work on a 6-month training and then you become whatever position you have trained for. Parenting; every single phase presents a new problem. Every child presents his or her problem. The problem of one child is totally different to another child. This is something that the parents want the children to know. So, actively participate as a parent. That is tip number two.

3. Leading by Example

The number one mechanism to influence your child positively is not through the schooling that you choose. It is not through the books that you read or put in your child's library. No. The number one mechanism that will influence your child is you. Your *akhlaq*. Your *mu'amalat*. Your interactions, how you treat other people. How you worship Allah s.w.t. The way you show yourself to be a mother or a father, a citizen, or a human being will rub off your child 100% more than anything else. Do not become so obsessed with things like where they go to school, for example, because schooling influences them only 5 to 10% of their behaviour and *akhlaq*. 90% of the child's overall philosophy, *akhlaq* and mannerisms originate from the household. Examine your relationship with your spouse. Examine the environment of the household. Correct yourself, and believe it or not, in correcting yourself, you will correct most of your children. This is why I said, rule number one is that there are no rules. The number one mechanism of fusing your children with good *akhlaq, iman* and *taqwa* is to manifest it in your own life. Do not expect an easy solution. "I throw my kid to the *madrasah* and he is going to come out a great person." No. The *madrasah* is not going to shape the child as much as you will. These weekend schools, the 2-hour *imam* who comes to your house to teach the Qur'an. That is not going to have as much influence as you will. Lead by example.

I want to give you an anecdote from my personal life and I ask refuge from Allah from any arrogance; Allah knows I am a sinner, Allah knows I am not boasting or bragging, I am just giving an example from my own life that even shocked me, about the influence of my parents. I know two or three people here from Houston who know my parents. My parents are, *alhamdulillāh*, still alive. May Allah give them a blissful long life. 85 years old, *alhamdulillāh*. My father is known in Houston as the person who was part of the first *masjid* in Texas back in the early 60s. My father was the General Secretary of the *masjid*. He was active in Islam, he has been active for fifty years, *alhamdulillāh*. He is an activist. He is not a scholar, but he is a person who loves Islam and has always been involved with the community. And, one of the things that I remember, I grew up in the 80s. The *masjid* was far from my house. Like 25 minutes' drive back then. We were not going to drive. One thing my father did, every single day without exception, when the *adhan* for Ṣalatul Maghrib comes, he would shut off the TV, he would call the whole family—my aunt, my grandmother, my brother—he would call everybody to a dedicated room for *muṣalla*, and we will pray Maghrib in *jamaah*. Even if we had guests over—even non-Muslim guests—he would say, "Please excuse us, we have to go for our prayer." If I have an Organic Chemistry exam the next day? Doesn't matter. He would call us, "Time to pray." We would pray. I grew up this way. In 1995, I went to Madinah. I spent 10 solid years in Madinah. *Alḥamdulillāh*, Allah blessed me that every single day, without exception, I prayed Maghrib and 'Isha' in the *masjid* of Prophet Muḥammad s.a.w., unless I was sick or travelling. Otherwise, as I said, even if I have exams, I would pray in the Ḥaram . This was my routine. After 'Asr, I would go to the Ḥaram , and sit there with my book, until after 'Isha'. Every day for ten years. Maghrib and 'Isha' in the Ḥaram . *Alḥamdulillāh*, I miss those days.

In 2005, I finished my Master's Degree and got accepted to Yale. By this time, Allah blessed me, and I had three kids; Ammar was five years old, and Yusuf and Sarah were toddlers. So for ten years, I have not been to Houston. And I did not have a car when I first moved, and the *masjid* was also far away. And *subḥānAllāh*, come Maghrib time, I felt an itch. And I said, maybe I should start praying Maghrib with my little kids. And every single day, I would give the *adhan*, and have my little Ammar; my Sarah was still in her diapers, and everybody would line up behind me and we would pray Maghrib. And to this day, when I am at home, all of our family comes together and we would pray Maghrib. I was shocked myself that I did not even know that something my father did throughout my life was latent in my heart. It was planted as a seed in my heart. When I came of age and had my own kids, what happened? It just came out. It just sprouted and became that tree that to this day, and I have no doubt, *insha'Allāh*, I am confident in Allah, *husnuzan billāh*, that when my sons and daughter become of that age, they are able to do the same with their kids because they saw their mother and father do the same. Because their father saw his mother and father do the same. This is what *tarbiyyah* is. You lead by example. You lead by being a role model. Let me give you another statistic on the negative side. And again I say this is negative but we should learn from it. I read a number of years ago a statistic that was surprising to me at that time. Around 70% of men who are abusive to their wives physically, come from households in which they saw their fathers abuse their mothers. Pause here, footnote: No man is a man who beats his wife. Our Prophet s.a.w. said:

> "How does anyone of you beat his wife as he beats the stallion camel and then he may embrace (sleep with) her?" (Ṣaḥīḥ al-Bukhari 6042)

How can anyone beat your wife, the way you would beat an animal? How could you? Where is your *qiwamah*?

In a *hadith*, our Prophet s.a.w. mentioned that a number of ladies complained to him s.a.w. that their husbands beat them. He s.a.w. said:

> "Many women have come to the family of Muhammad complaining about their husbands. These men are not the best among you." (Sunan Abi Dawud 2146)

He shamed them in public as he gave a *khutbah* on Friday. Aishah r.a. said, the Prophet s.a.w. never once raised his hand against a lady or a servant. In a society in which beating your wife is the default and norm—every household beat his wife—but the Prophet s.a.w. never once raised his hand. Husbands, please follow the *sunnah* of the Prophet s.a.w.

75% of men who abused their wives saw their fathers abuse their mothers. I first read that 4 years ago. I was genuinely shocked. Why, may I ask you? Put yourself as a fifteen-year-old teenager. Imagine, hypothetically, your father hitting your mother. Who you would side with as a fifteen-year-old? Instantaneously, the mother. Any man would say the mother since the sense of *qiwamah* is still there. This is *qiwamah* by the way, you want to protect your loved ones. You would automatically side with your mother, to protect her. Maybe someone would even stand in front of the mother and say, "Hey, you have to hit me before you hit her." A teenager would do that. The anger is there. "How dare you hit my mother" So, when I read this statistic, I was shocked because I am a man. I know how a man would feel if he saw anyone, even his father, lift his hand on his mother. *How dare you do that?* So how can a fifteen-year-old who is sympathising with a woman getting beaten—he turns thirty-five—becomes the one who beats his wife? And not the one who defends the one who is getting beaten? Do you understand my conundrum? How can that happen? And of course, the answer is self-evidence which came to me after contemplation. Intellectually, the man knows this is wrong. But emotionally, what *tarbiyyah* had he seen in his household, when he was younger? He had seen that when a man gets angry, he beats on the woman. He grew up that way. Even if his brain tells him his action is wrong, his emotions kick in and the *tarbiyyah* of the household has a negative impact on him. He would do something that his eyes have seen what he has been growing up with regardless of his brain acknowledging that the action is wrong at so many levels. So, my point is, husbands and wives, mothers and fathers, your *akhlaq* will rub off on your children inevitably. Lead by example. That is the number one mechanism.

I will tell you anecdotally from my own life. I grew up in a time when Islam was very young in America and there were only one or two masjids. It was a very different world.

There was no internet at that time. But I will tell you from my own experience, all of my colleagues and friends and acquaintances who came from stable and loving religious households *eventually* came back to religion. Why do I say eventually? A lot of times, young men and women, teenagers, and college-aged kids, might veer left or right. They might go astray, and get involved in society but I have seen in my own eyes, people that I thought were hopeless, later on in college, living lifestyles far from Islam, but it is just a phase. One day, they grow out of it and they get married. And then they have children. That is when the real change comes. Once the person has children, *subḥānAllāh*. It is as if a new person is born. But that is not the case. It is the child coming out again. The child is seeing the parents raising him or her. That person is rediscovered. Because now he or she realises that: "I have a responsibility. I have to do something to protect this child and what role model this person has?" *Me.*

If you still have your parents, maybe it is not too late to tell your parents: "Thank you. You did a good job raising me." If not, please acknowledge that our parents actually did their best in raising us. Maybe when we were 18 we were angry at our parents. But by the time we reach the age of 28, we know how much our parents sacrifice for us. It is human nature. So, dear parents, always remember you are in it for the long run. Do not have a debate with your son or daughter thinking that you need to win today. Listen to me carefully, next time you are shouting at your son or daughter, understand that this shouting match will have repercussions for your grandchildren. Even if you have to lose the battle to win the war, think long-term, not short-term. Your *akhlaq*, your *tarbiyyah*, and your mannerisms will impact generations to come.

4. Cut them some slacks

One of the biggest issues I find in our time is the disconnection that parents have from the culture of our times. This is especially true of this generation. Most people above the age of 35 really and truly are not aware of the influence of social media. They do not know the difference between Snapchat and Instagram. They do not understand the positive and negative sides of Facebook or any type of app that has the potential to reach out and influence your children. And I know it is scary and terrifying; it is a new world but you are responsible for these kids. How to deal with this? *Cut them some slacks*. I grew up in the 80s and there were no internet or cell phones back then. Kids nowadays could not imagine a world without those facilities. When I was telling my children about this, my daughter, she was nine at the time, she was like, "Was there electricity when you were growing up? She could not imagine how could life happens without the internet, you know, making her question if there was even electricity or cars during those times. So they cannot imagine a world without these amenities. Frankly, sometimes, for me, I thought it too. How did I live without a cell phone? I went through college without a cell phone. The internet came out during my last year of university. There was no global world wide web, it was just a few websites here and there. That was it. So I caught the last phase of the "prehistoric" era. I used to know how to live without the internet. Even though these days I cannot. My point is dear parents, those of you who grew up in the 80s or those who are older than me, in the 70s or 60s. Didn't you do things back then behind your parents? Things they didn't know of or approve of? We all did. Can you imagine if you have the internet back then, what you would have done? Can you imagine if you had access towards what your children have access to? I would thank Allah for my case. That I did not have that access. But it makes me terrified that my kids do.

So here I pose two important points. Number one, your children are going to do more than you did. Because they have more to do. It is like throwing your child into the water and saying, "Don't get wet." It is not their fault. This is their world. They are living in it. They did not choose to be born in a world of the internet and Facebook and Snapchat and YouTube. It is not their fault. Cut them some slacks and remember that you did not have the types of freedom and potential to unleash the online power as they do now. So your mistakes were controlled. But their mistakes are going to be more than that because of their resources and capability. This is human nature. Then this leads me to my second point. Whose job it is to monitor them? It is *yours*. You need to take an active role. Learn, ask and do not be naive. Do not live in a bubble. Ask your friends or your colleague. What is going on? What is Instagram? What are Snapchat and Facebook? What can I do to put parental controls? Parents, there are parental controls on Facebook. Did you know that? You as the parents have the right to give your children a "child Facebook account". Make sure you are monitoring your children's page. Especially until they are teenagers. I opined that it is foolish for a parent to give unfiltered access to the internet to their children. You have no idea of the filth that is two clicks away on the internet. You need to put software—if you do not know how—call your friends; everybody has an IT expert friend, right? Bring him over to install the software for you. There is paid and free software.

Another tradition in my household is that I am going to be strict with them if their age has not reached adolescence. But once they are teenagers, you have to give them more slack in the reality. In my household, for the youngest children, the computer is in the living room. They do not need a private computer. Everybody is there, everybody is walking in and out. Fun fact: There is a hidden history bar on internet browsers. Learn that. If the history is deleted, think about why and who is deleting it. There are things that you have to learn and find out. If you find something inappropriate, **DO NOT** go berserk and ballistic. You might have done the same. No, don't tell me you won't. You would have if you are 13 years old and you have access to the internet. Ultimately, react with compassion for the long run. Speak to them at their intelligence level. Remember to always try to understand the time that we are living in and take charge of this modern technology to the best of your knowledge.

5. Spend quality time

This is especially to fathers. Dear parents who are earning, primarily, fathers. Dear breadwinners in the households. When you start your career, understandably, you have to give a hundred and ten per cent; you have to work hard, and you have to rise up in the company. *Inshā'Allāh*, at the same time, Allah bless you with children. Now, there will come in time when there will be a fork in the road. You are earning enough to get by. So you think you could get a little more money if you give more hours at work. But this comes with a price. *You have to spend less time with the kids*. Every one of us, there will come a time in our life when we will have to make a choice: more time for our career or more time for our children. If we go to our career, *shaytan* and *nafs* will come and say, "I can take care of my children better because I have more money." Remember, the bulk of a man's determination is to increase the status of his family. Never forget that. When you get irritated at your husband toiling in the office, realise, the chances are he is toiling because of you. But what husbands don't understand: husbands, wives and children—a time will come when they need your presence more than they need your wallet. So my fifth point: spend quality time rather than extra money with your children than upon your children. Time versus money. Now, *what is the ratio?* This is up to you. I cannot tell you. Every family is different. *When the decision has to be made?* You know best. I cannot tell you that either. But every one of you will go through a time when your children need your presence more than they need the extra cake. The extra gadget. The extra, surplus cash. And when that time comes, prioritise your family over your extra career. I am not saying, "Quit your job." I am saying, "You don't need that promotion. Spend that extra hour every day at home." Simply being with the children. That's all. Being with them. Interacting with them. Being a presence in their lives. That is what they need. Money will come. Believe it or not, money will come. You will be empty nesters again. Your kids will grow up and leave the household. Right now, my eldest has already gone to university. This will be followed by the second, third and fourth. Then, *done*. Literally, those years go by in the twinkling of an eye. *SubḥānAllāh*, that's life. You will have plenty of time for money. But you only have one opportunity for your kids. So spend that quality time with them. And listen to this beautiful *ḥadith* of our Prophet s.a.w. reported in the Muslim and Ahmad. Our Prophet s.a.w. said:

> "Any act devoid of the remembrance of Allah is a waste of time…" (Sunan Abi Dawud 2513)

Everything that we do in absence of the *dhikr* of Allah, and *dhikr* of Allah means anything related to Islam. Qur'an, knowledge, *ṣalah*, *ʿilm*—anything. It is a waste of time. I mean let's be brutally honest, you watch an hour of Netflix; it is a waste of time. And then the Prophet s.a.w. said: "Except four things." (Sunan Abi Dawud 2513). I don't want to go to all four, but I will just mention one. One of those four is a man playing (*mulaʿabah*) with his family. This is a *ḥadith* of the Prophet s.a.w. He used the word *mulaʿabah* meaning playing, having a fun time; or going on a picnic. Even if you don't do the *dhikr* of Allah, there is worship going on right there. What a beautiful *ḥadith*, dear readers. A man spending a loving time with his family is blessed even though there is no actual worship. And the reason for this goes back to my point number 5, quality time. It is a part of the bond of being a father or a mother. Establishing love, being a figure and a presence in your children's life.

6. Connect with Family, Friends and the Community

What are the most important things we need to do to raise our children? There is a famous saying: It takes a village to raise a child. This is true. You need to get help from other people. So, point number six; connect with family and friends and the community. That will help you with a good environment. It is your job to monitor your friends because their children will influence your children. A man follows the religion of his friends—as the Prophet s.a.w. said—so be careful whose religion you are following. Be careful whom you befriend. If there are people whom you invite over who are not a positive influence on you, then why would you invite them over, in front of your children? Why do you have relationships with people who are not influencing you in a good manner? You need to choose your circle of friends. You cannot choose your colleague at work. That is fine. But you can all choose whom you invite over on occasion. With whom do you have family dinners? With whom do you go out for picnics? With whom do you establish bonds of actual and genuine camaraderie and friendship with? You decide that. If the people you choose are not the people who are well-mannered and have good *akhlaq* and righteousness, then it is not wise that you influence your own children indirectly through them. It takes a village to raise a child. In the American context, one thing that I put under this point is to live close to a *masjid* and frequent the *masjid* constantly. Take your children to the masjid. Make it a family experience. Fathers, take your sons to the *masjid*. Take them to religious gatherings. Introduce them to the scholars and *ʿulamaʾ*. Let them see a positive role model. This is a part of your *tarbiyyah*. Again, it takes a village to raise a child. So you choose the village that will surround your child. As Americans, we are surrounded by non-Muslims. Therefore, you need to make sure that your child is surrounded by Islam. And when the country is majority Muslim, you need to make sure that your child is surrounded by *practising* Muslims. By Muslims who are observing the rituals. By Muslims who are showing them what it means to be a Muslim. You see, here's the point. Dear brothers and sisters, Islam is not just theoretical. It is a lived, experiential reality. Your child will see more than what they read in a book. Your child will absorb through osmosis more than what they absorb going to a *halaqah* in the *masjid*. When they see the *akhlaq* of the elders. When they see *rahmah* manifested. That will have an impact on them much more than memorising the Islamic lessons they learned in grade

5. So the lived experiential reality of Islam must be shown through you and your friends and colleague that you choose to come to your house and whose house you go to.

Last but definitely not least, dear brothers and sisters.

7. Make *du'a'* constantly

Make sure that you make *du'a'* for your children constantly. *SubḥānAllāh*, there are so many prophetic *du'a'* in the Qur'an about children.

...رَبَّنَا هَبْ لَنَا مِنْ أَزْوَٰجِنَا وَذُرِّيَّـٰتِنَا قُرَّةَ أَعْيُنٍ وَٱجْعَلْنَا لِلْمُتَّقِينَ إِمَامًا ﴿٧٤﴾

...Rabbanā hablanā min ajwājinā wa zurriyyātinā qurrata aʿyunin wajʿalnā lilmuttaqīna imāmā

...Our Lord, grant us from among our wives and offspring comfort to our eyes and make us a leader [i.e., example] for the righteous. (al-Furqan, 25:74)

Children

رَبِّ ٱجْعَلْنِى مُقِيـمَ ٱلصَّلَوٰةِ وَمِن ذُرِّيَّتِى ۚ رَبَّنَا وَتَقَبَّلْ دُعَآءِ ۞ رَبَّنَا ٱغْفِـرْ لِى وَلِوَٰلِـدَىَّ وَلِلْمُؤْمِنِينَ يَـوْمَ يَقُـومُ ٱلْحِسَـابُ ۞

Rabbij'alnī muqīmaṣṣalāti wamin zurriyyati Rabbanā wataqabbal du'a'. Rabbanāghfirlī waliwālidayya walilmu'nīna yauma yaqūmul-ḥisāb.

My Lord, make me an establisher of prayer, and [many] from my descendants. Our Lord, and accept my supplication. Our Lord, forgive me and my parents and the believers the Day the account is established. (Ibrahim, 14:40-41)

...رَبِّ أَوْزِعْنِى أَنْ أَشْكُرَ نِعْمَتَكَ ٱلَّتِى أَنْعَمْتَ عَلَىَّ وَعَلَىٰ وَٰلِدَىَّ وَأَنْ أَعْمَلَ صَٰلِحًا تَرْضَىٰهُ وَأَصْلِحْ لِى فِى ذُرِّيَّتِى ۖ إِنِّى تُبْتُ إِلَيْكَ وَإِنِّى مِنَ ٱلْمُسْلِمِينَ ۞

...Rabbī auzighnī an ashkura ni'matakallatī an'amta 'alayya wa'alā wālidayya wa'an a'mala ṣaliḥān taḍāhu wa'aṣliḥ lī fī zurriyyatī innī tubtu ilayka wainnī minalmuslimīn

...My Lord, enable me to be grateful for Your favour which You have bestowed upon me and upon my parents and to work righteousness of which You will approve and make righteous for me my offspring. Indeed, I have repented to You, and indeed, I am of the Muslims. (al-Ahqaf, 45:15)

Most of them are upon the tongue of the Prophet s.a.w. Allah is encouraging you in the Qur'an; "Make *du'a'* for your children." Constantly make *du'a'* for your children. Our Prophet s.a.w. said, "Three are the *du'a'* Allah s.w.t. never rejects. Number one: *Du'a'* of a parent to the child. It is a guarantee from Allah that the *du'a'* will be accepted. Parents, when was the last time—when there was no crisis in your or your child's life, and a time that commonly eases, and just out of love—you raise your hands up to Allah and you make *du'a'* for your kids? If you are not going to make *du'a'* for your children, what does that show? You cannot even raise your hands to Allah and ask Him to give you children who are righteous? To make your children pious? To make them have good *akhlaq* and manners? And by the way, making *du'a'* does not just have the *barakah* of Allah; where Allah's blessing is coming down, but making *du'a'* reminds you that you have a responsibility. Making *du'a* reminds you that: "Hey, these are my kids. I better take care of them." It is also self-monitoring and self-reflection. Parents, if you have all the pleasure of this world, but you are not keeping an eye on your children's faith and manners, what use is money? What use is anything else? In *surah* al-Kahf verse 46, Allah mentions, "Wealth and children are what make life beautiful." Allah says that in the Qur'an. Children are also the comfort of the eyes. Children are what makes you proud and ironically what brings you the most frustration as well because you love them so much. Your children—if you are not even making *du'a'* for them, *subḥānAllāh*, for whom are you making *du'a*? So make *du'a'* for your kids. *Constantly* make *du'a'* for them. Realise that *du'a'* might even be accepted after you are gone. You might not even see the results of that *du'a'*.

I will conclude this point with a personal anecdote. It goes back to one of my close family friends. There is a family friend. He is younger than me but I grew up with him. His father sent him to the *madrasah* and his father moved next to the *masjid*. They would walk to the *masjid* five times a day and he literally purchased a house in America—an apartment—which has walking distance to the *masjid*. Sent his kids to *tahfiz* schools. The kids started memorising the Qur'an. The sisters were wearing *ḥijab* and the brothers wearing beards. Such a religious family, *masha'Allāh*. Mind you, this was in America. This person is the youngest son. He is ten years younger than me. When he reached 15, he came across some bad friends and left the madrasah. Did drugs, alcohol and women. Fell out of high school. Got his GED. Then he went to the university and the situation got much worse than that. Imagine, the parents of this very religious family are practising Muslims and living next to the *masjid*, but this young friend of mine, publicly announced that he is a *murtad*. Left Islam. This really hurts me because this is my family friend. I grew up with him. His parents are the humblest and sweetest people you could ever imagine. Obviously, they were heartbroken. One day, I was just walking out from a *halaqah*. Then I saw him. *Astaghfirullāh*, he was making fun of me. He went, "How long will you preach fairy tales to your audiences?" He mocked me and that really hurt. My thought was, "This is your level now? From the *tahfiz* school to this?" May Allah guides us all. I was just a family friend to him, but the scene hurts me deeply. So you can imagine how his parents felt. The father constantly makes *du'a'*. He almost got depression. Eventually, the father passed away. *SubḥānAllāh*. Suddenly, that brother texted me, "Shaykh, I need to talk to you." Suddenly, he called me Shaykh. Where does this come from? He said, "I need to come to you. Give me your address." I said, "You're in Houston." I was in Tennessee at that time. He said, "I'm going to fly down to you." So I gave him my address since he is a family friend of mine. He flew down the next day to come see me, the week his father passed away. He came to my house, and he broke down, sobbing and crying. He said, "I ask Allah to forgive me. What can I do to make up for the pain and hurt that I caused my father?" Then he said the *shahadah* in front of me; in my living room. Then he said, "I need to dedicate my life now to make up for my father for the hurt and pain I've caused. *SubhānAllāh*, his father's death triggered the latent *iman*. You see, this goes back to my previous point. There will be a phase—a teenage phase—which will get worse and involves drugs, alcohol, and woman, and arrogance would come as well. At that time, you build a false wall and you think you know yourself. In his case, it was too late since the father has passed away. *But the father never stopped making du'a'.* Even on his deathbed, he is still making *du'a'* for his son. The father did not live to see the effects of *du'a'* but we did. All of us did. I told him, he needs to repent to Allah, go perform *'umrah* and *ḥajj* on behalf of his father, and organise a charity. Now he is completely changed and he has become the son the father would have loved in a different way, after the demise of his father. My point, dear parents, is when you fight your battles with your teenagers, don't just think of winning today. Don't think of the battle of here and now. Understand that their world is different than yours and time has changed. Understand and cut the kid some slack. Give him much more leeway than your parents had given you. And remember that in the world that we live in, compassion and mercy will win much more than strictness and harshness. Love will always win. Even if it means you have to give some liberty that you don't like right now. Because the ultimate battle is not one day, it is the life of the child and the life of your grandchild after that. So make a lot of *du'a'* with a lot of love. Then you leave the rest to Allah s.w.t. because again, going back to rule number: there are no rules. Nuh a.s.; can anyone say he is a bad father? No. But his son became a *kafir*. You can have all of the things but the child goes away. 'Asiyah is married to Fir'awn and in that household, she has become the best of the best. You can only do so much. Then you leave to Allah the rest. As long as you have tried and you put in the effort. Then on Judgment Day, at least you have a clean conscience and slate. *Insha'Allāh*, generally speaking as we said these are general rules, if you did it properly, it does have a positive impact on the next generation. We ask Allah s.w.t. to guide us and our children after us and our grandchildren after them. We ask Allah s.w.t. to make *iman* stronger in our hearts and our children's hearts. We ask Allah s.w.t. that all of us and our progeny and their progeny after them with the love of the Qur'an and the love of the Prophet s.a.w. We ask Allah s.w.t. to make us and our children from those who are established in their *ṣalah* and pay their *zakah* and those who fast during Ramadan. We ask Allah s.w.t. to make us and our children role models to the people around us and to make us and our children those who walk in the footstep of the Prophet s.a.w. We ask Allah s.w.t. for us to live as Muslims and to die as Mu'min and to be resurrected as the pious and the righteous and the martyrs and the prophets. *Āmīn.*

Questions and Answers

1. **In the Qur'an, there is an instance where Allah said that your children and wealth are distractions for you. So I do want to be closer to Allah, by the means of my children, but I do experience how children can also be a distraction for you to pray or read the Qur'an. So how do you balance that?**

   Answer: This is *surah* at-Taghabun verse 15. *Innamā amwālakum wa awlādukum* **fitnah**. *Fitnah* here is not a distraction, but it is a trial. Your wealth and children are a test and you can pass the test with flying colours because passing the test makes you raise a rank. You passed your medical exam, you become a doctor. You passed the legal test, you become a lawyer. You pass, and you climb a rank up. But you can also fail the test and go down. So your family and your wealth are a means of becoming closer to Allah s.w.t. or, we seek Allah's refuge, *āmīn*, distancing yourself from Allah s.w.t. This is how we should translate the verse. This does not mean that you should run away from them because they are a distraction. It means that you embrace Islam and you want to pass the test through them—your children and wealth. This is what the verse means, *insha'Allāh*.

2. **I am a mother of two, a nine and a six-year-old. My six-year-old daughter is a special needs kid. She's deaf. So, do you have any advice for us, for special needs parents?**

Answer: First and foremost, realise that Allah s.w.t. loves you. And because He loves you, He wants to raise your rank. And because He wants to raise your ranks, He has gifted you with a gift, that requires extra love and patience. Our Prophet s.a.w. said, "When Allah s.w.t. loves someone, He tests her or him. And the more beloved they are to Allah, the more they are tested. The most beloved to Allah are the prophets and those who are after them and those after them. The more difficulties that you have in this *dunya, inshā'Allāhu ta'ala,* this means the more Allah loves you. So you have to turn to Allah s.w.t. and try your best to use your difficulties to come closer to Allah s.w.t. As for some practical advice, obviously, I am not a special needs therapist. I cannot give you such advice. But I can tell you religiously and spiritually, *lā yukallifullāhu nafsan illā wus'aha.* This means that a child with special needs does not burden them more than their needs and what they are able to do. Do not aspect them to do the same things other children are doing. And Allah s.w.t. will not punish them for something they are not capable of doing. Especially in the issue of hearing and not being able to hear. This is definitely a big test for you and your child. In fact, in the days before there were sign languages, there is a *ḥadith* that said, "One of the people that Allah would forgive on Judgment Day is the one who is not able to hear, someone who is deaf. And then he who said, "O' Allah, Islam came but I could not hear anything." So Allah s.w.t. will forgive him. We also believe by the way, when Allah s.w.t. takes away something, He gives something else in return. We firmly believe that if Allah has taken something away from you or your family or your loved ones, Allah has given you something else that He has not given other people. So, Allah is the Most Just. And whenever he takes something, he gives multiple things in return. So, rather than concentrating on the negatives, always look at the positives as well. Look at the blessings Allah s.w.t. has given you and realise that taking care of someone who requires extra care; is a reward for you. A means of *shafa'ah* for you, a means for your *Jannah*. This is the beauty of our religion, you can earn *Jannah* even through the smallest deeds people do not appreciate and realise. You can earn *Jannah* in the privacy of your home, by your mercy and compassion to your own family and to your special needs child. So I ask Allah to give you *ṣabr* and *tawfiq*. I ask Allah to give you the mercy, love, compassion, and patience that is required. These days we have so much potential to teach various things to special needs children unlike in the past. So, obviously take advantage of that. May Allah s.w.t. make your affairs very easy for you.

3. **My question is about the Prophet s.a.w. He s.a.w. must have been very busy. So with limited time, how was the interaction between the Prophet and his children and how frequent is the interaction?**

Answer: Believe it or not, I have mentioned a lot in my *sirah* lectures, but we do not have too many details about this. The reason is that all of his daughters passed away in his life except for Fatimah. And Fatimah passed away six months after he passed away. We do not have much information about how he interacted with his daughters, of course, his sons passed away when he was younger. So again, we have very little information about that. But what we do have are beautiful anecdotes of Hasan and Husayn. We do have plenty of stories about the grandchildren. Because those are the ones who lived longer. But regarding the Prophet's immediate children, we have very little. What a test for our Prophet s.a.w. Not only his father, his mother, his uncle, his grandfather—every one of his children, he buried himself. Seven children, six of whom he buried himself. Can you imagine? Even on his deathbed, he said to Fatimah, "That you shall be the first in my family to die." And she passed away six months after him. The Prophet was indeed tested. But your question is beautiful, the answer is underlying with Hasan and Husayn, not about the immediate children.

4. **I would like to seek your advice. We have in our home two daughters whom we have adopted. And both of them carry their original father's name. So it is two different names. And often people question us about what will happen because it will be discrimination and bullying in school. What would be your advice because now they are coming to two and three and we would, *inshā'Allāh* start school for them soon?**

Answer: Firstly, may Allah s.w.t. bless you for taking care of two children and their *tarbiyyah* and adopting them. One of our biggest blunders of Islamic literature was that back in the 70s or 60s when the first *fiqh* book was translated into English, it stated that adoption is *ḥaram* in Islam. And this translation continues to perpetuate throughout the 70s, 80s and 90s until they became this notion among English-speaking Westerners. So people in America and Canada and England think that adoption is *haram* . This is a mistake. The *haram* concept is the Arabic word *tabanni*. It is to claim that a child is your biological child when it is not. This is *tabanni* and it is *haram* . Our Prophet s.a.w. had practised *tabanni*, as he had taken Zayd bin Harithah, and said, "This is Zayd bin Muḥammad." This is *tabanni*. Then Allah revealed in *surah* al-Ahzab verses 4 & 5, "*Call them by their fathers.*" And so *tabanni* was abrogated. It is not allowed. Permissible adoption is when you take somebody's child and you tell them when they are older, "That's your real parents. You have been adopted." You raised them as if your child, love-wise. Not as if they are your child, name-wise. This is one of the best of good deeds in the eyes of Allah s.w.t.; to raise an orphan. To protect and care for them. Our Prophet s.a.w. said:

"I and the one who takes the responsibility of an orphan will be in Paradise thus, and he joined his middle finger and forefinger." (Sunan Abi Dawud 5150)

This is an adoption that is positive. There really is nothing wrong with it, it is actually one of the greatest of good deeds and I encourage all of you who have wealth and means to take of orphans in your home. Treat them with the same love and compassion and education that you gave your own children. The only difference is that you need to tell them when they are able to understand, that, their biological parents are so-and-so. Or if you don't know, then you say, you don't know, we took you from an adoption centre. In America, there is actually a very good series of children's books that are meant to teach adopted kids even when they are two years old. There are pictures about "Where I come from", and then some of them are kids being picked up from the orphanage, some from the hospitals. So you teach them at this age, such that, when the child is ten, if he or she receives the news about them being adopted, they would not be shocked. They will understand. You are theirs *psychologically*. Therapists have done this now that you slowly feed information that helps them understand by the time they are older, that they are adopted. The only caveat is that you cannot hide their biological parents when they are able to understand when they are old enough. Also, they will not be your *maḥram* technically, unless there was fostering. Then, *alḥamdulillāh* if fostering was done then they are *maḥram* to you. I would like to also say that parents, sisters and brothers, do not allow the fear of non-*mahramiah* to stop you from taking care of an orphan. There is another major problem, if the child is not your *maḥram*, OK, it is better than the child being in an orphanage, right? I mean, again, let's be brutally honest here. So what if your *ḥijab* slips off after 20 years or when he is a 20-year-old? So what? Biologically, he is not your child but psychologically he thinks you are the mother. Allah is not going to punish you for a slip of the *ḥijab* but Allah is going to reward you Jannah for taking the kid out of the orphanage and raising him. Please, prioritise. Don't make a trivial issue like your *ḥijab* an impediment to earning *Jannah* through an orphan. *WAllāhi*, I'm amazed that some people don't want to adopt because they say, "I'll have to wear *ḥijab* when the kid is 20." I swear to you, if you don't wear your *ḥijab*, and take care of the child, it is a bigger good deed and a bigger means of *shafaʿah* than not taking care of the child thinking that, "I'll have to wear *ḥijab* when he grows up." Think of the pros and cons. Do you know what I'm saying? So, of course, he is not your *maḥram*. But if it happens that you don't wear your *ḥijab* then OK, it is not the end of the world. You took care of the child, you raised an orphan. That is your *Jannah* right there. So, don't make a technicality a reason to stop a massive amount of good coming to your household. If you are able to, before the age of two, adopt the child and then lactate and feed him even by medication, then *alḥamdulillāh*, you have no issue of *maḥram*, *inshā'Allāh*

5. In Islam, which is better, a joint family or a nuclear family?

Answer: Islam does not have an explicit verdict on this. But culture and society have shown that there are many positive and negative sides to both. Generally speaking, the positives outweigh the negatives of a joint family system. Nonetheless, in the society that we live in, globally, a nuclear family is becoming the norm and Allah commands us in the Qur'an to treat our spouses according to culture, *bil ma'ruf* or according to *'uruf*. Therefore in our time, it is reasonable for a woman to request for a separate domicile once she gets married—I speak for the American context because my *fatwa* is related to my land. It might not be reasonable for 100 years in many lands. 100 years ago, it would have been understood that she gets a room in a larger household. In our time and Western culture, in particular, it is reasonable for her to demand her own residence because that is her de facto effective norm across the Western hemisphere. What I suggest—by the way, I am very thankful to Allah in my particular case—this year my father and my mother moved in with me and we are now living in an entire household *alḥamdulillāh*. But I will be honest with you that it is *very, very* atypical in America. It is also because most families are not able financially to afford that. They do not have a house like that. So what I suggest is the next best thing: find houses or apartments that are as close as reasonable. Because the wife does have the right to expect privacy in her domicile and the husband does have the obligation to take care of his mother and father. So, we reconcile that by saying, "Try to have both obligations being done without infringing the rights of the other." But we have no Qur'anic verses or *ḥadith* regarding this so we deal with it according to the culture as Islam has prescribed us to.

Glossary

Glossary

1. *Adhan*: Calling to prayers

2. *Akhirah*: Hereafter

3. *Akhlaq*: Manners

4. *Ayah*: Verse

5. *Darajah*: Degree

6. *Dhikr*: Remembrance of Allah s.w.t.

7. *Dunya*: World

8. *Du'a'*: Invocations

9. *Fiqh*: Rulings

10. *Fitrah*: Nature

11. *Ḥadith*: A collection of traditions containing sayings of the Prophet Muhammad s.a.w.

12. *Ḥajj*: Pilgrimage

13. *Ḥalal*: Permissible

14. *Halaqah*: Religious circle

15. *Ḥaram*: Not permissible

16. *Ḥijab*: Head coverings for women

17. *Ikhlaṣ*: Sincerity

18. *Imam*: A title for Muslim leaders

19. *Iman*: Faith

20. *Jama'ah*: Congregation

21. *Jannah*: Paradise

22. *La'nah*: Curse

23. *Madrasah*: A college for Islamic instructions

24. *Maḥr*: Dowry

25. *Maḥram*: A family member with whom marriage would be considered permanently unlawful

26. *Masjid*: Mosque

27. *Mata'*: Temporary

28. *Mawaddah*: Tender love

29. *Murtad*: An apostate from Islam

30. *Muṣalla*: Prayer room (usually smaller than a *masjid*)

31. *Mu'amalat*: Transactions or dealings

32. *Nafs*: Desire

33. *Nikaḥ*: Marriage

34. *Niyyah*: Intention

35. *Qadr*: Fate

36. *Qawwam*: Protector, maintainer

37. *Qiwamah*: Protection, maintenance

38. *Rahmah*: Compassion

39. *Ṣabr*: Patience

40. *Ṣaḥabah*: Companions

41. *Sajdah*: Prostration

42. *Sakinah*: Peace

43. *Ṣalah*: Prayer

44. *Ṣalatul Maghrib*: Prayer in the evening; during the dusk

45. *Shafa'ah*: Intercession

46. *Shaghaf*: Lustful love

47. *Shahadah*: Profession of faith

48. *Shari'ah*: Islamic canonical law

49. *Shayṭan*: Satan

50. *Sirah*: the study of the life of the Prophet s.a.w.

51. *Sunnah*: Traditions of the Prophet s.a.w.

52. *Tabanni*: Adopting a child and admitting the child as their own by putting their own name to the child

53. *Tafsir*: Translation

54. *Tahfiz*: A school for memorising the Qur'an

55. *Taqwa*: Piety

56. *Tarbiyyah*: Education or upbringing

57. *Tawfiq*: Ability to succeed

58. *Wajib*: Compulsory

59. *Zakah*: Almsgiving

60. *Zina*: Adornment

61. *Ibadah*: Worship

62. *Ilm*: Knowledge

63. *Ulama²*: Scholars

64. *Umrah*: Non-mandatory pilgrimage